SUPER EASY SONGBOOK

TOP HITS

ISBN 978-1-5400-6258-1

Visit Hal Leonard Online at
www.halleonard.com

Contact us:
Hal Leonard
7777 West Bluemound Road
Milwaukee, WI 53213
Email: info@halleonard.com

In Europe, contact:
Hal Leonard Europe Limited
42 Wigmore Street
Marylebone, London, W1U 2RN
Email: info@halleonardeurope.com

In Australia, contact:
Hal Leonard Australia Pty. Ltd.
4 Lentara Court
Cheltenham, Victoria, 3192 Australia
Email: info@halleonard.com.au

Welcome to the *Super Easy Songbook* series!

This unique collection will help you play your favorite songs quickly and easily. Here's how it works:

- Play the simplified melody with your right hand. Letter names appear inside each note to assist you.

- There are no key signatures to worry about! If a sharp ♯ or flat ♭ is needed, it is shown beside the note each time.

- There are no page turns, so your hands never have to leave the keyboard.

- If two notes are connected by a tie ⌣, hold the first note for the combined number of beats. (The second note does not show a letter name since it is not re-struck.)

- Add basic chords with your left hand using the provided keyboard diagrams. Chord voicings have been carefully chosen to minimize hand movement.

- The left-hand rhythm is up to you, and chord notes can be played together or separately. Be creative!

- If the chords sound muddy, move your left hand an octave* higher. If this gets in the way of playing the melody, move your right hand an octave higher as well.

  * *An octave spans eight notes. If your starting note is C, the next C to the right is an octave higher.*

--------- ALSO AVAILABLE ---------

Hal Leonard Student Keyboard Guide HL00296039

Key Stickers HL00100016

Dancing with a Stranger

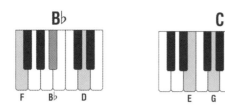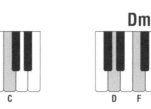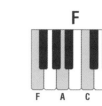

Words and Music by Sam Smith,
Tor Hermansen, Mikkel Eriksen,
Normani Hamilton and James Napier

Moderate Dance groove

I don't wan-na be a-lone to-night. It's pret-ty clear that I'm not o-ver you. I'm still think-in' 'bout the things you do, so I don't wan-na be a-lone to-night, a-lone to-night, a-lone to-night. Can you light the fire? I need some-bod-y who can

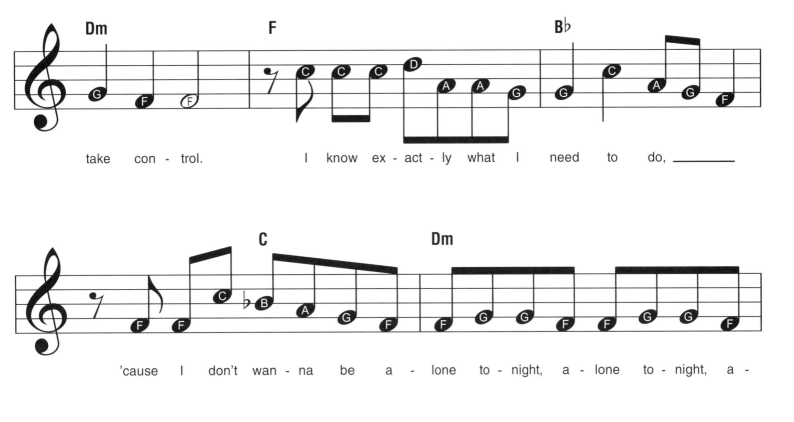

take con - trol. I know ex - act - ly what I need to do, _____

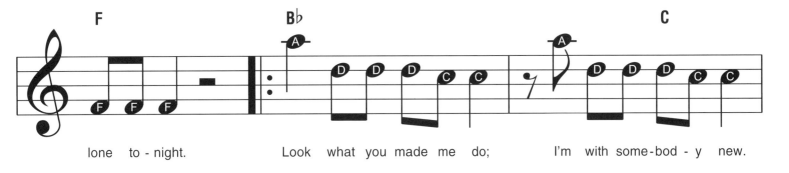

'cause I don't wan - na be a - lone to - night, a - lone to - night, a -

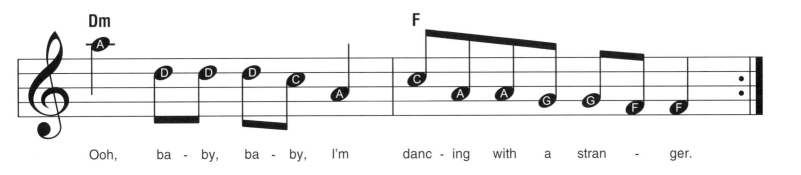

lone to - night. Look what you made me do; I'm with some - bod - y new.

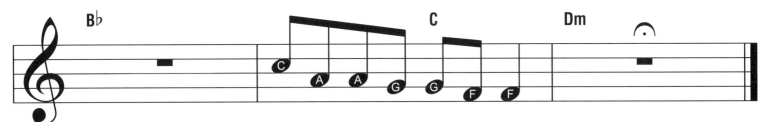

Ooh, ba - by, ba - by, I'm danc - ing with a stran - ger.

Danc - ing with a stran - ger.

Despacito

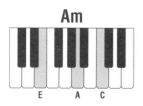
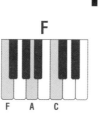
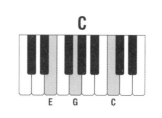
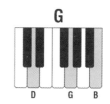

Words and Music by Luis Fonsi,
Erika Ender, Justin Bieber,
Jason Boyd, Marty James Garton
and Ramón Ayala

Moderate Latin beat

Des - pa - ci - to. Quie - ro res - pi - rar tu cue - llo des - pa -
ci - to. Quie - ro des - nu - dar - te a be - sos des - pa -

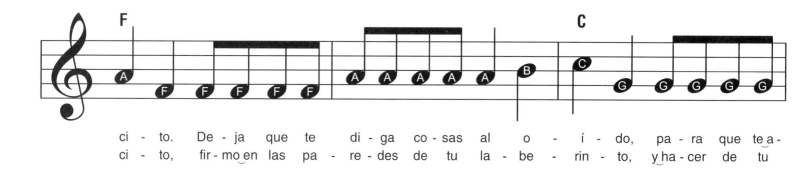

ci - to. De - ja que te di - ga co - sas al o - í - do, pa - ra que te a -
ci - to, fir - mo en las pa - re - des de tu la - be - rin - to, y ha - cer de tu

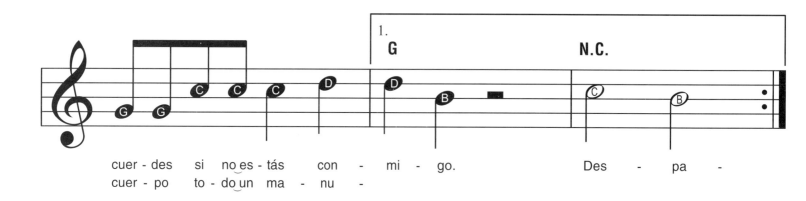

cuer - des si no es - tás con - mi - go. Des - pa -
cuer - po to - do un ma - nu -

Feel It Still

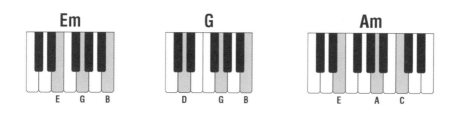

Words and Music by John Gourley,
Zach Carothers, Jason Sechrist,
Eric Howk, Kyle O'Quin,
Brian Holland, Freddie Gorman,
Georgia Dobbins, Robert Bateman,
William Garrett, John Hill and Asa Taccone

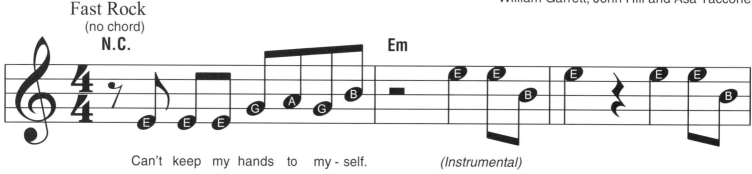

Can't keep my hands to my-self. *(Instrumental)*

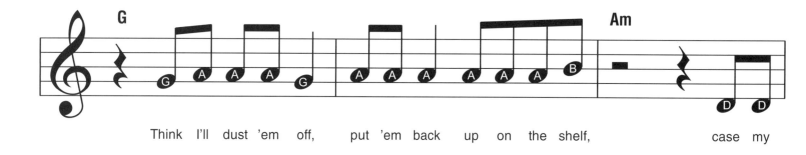

Think I'll dust 'em off, put 'em back up on the shelf, case my

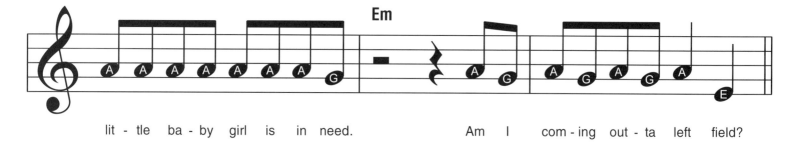

lit-tle ba-by girl is in need. Am I com-ing out-ta left field?

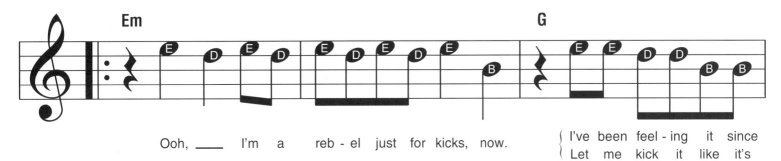

Ooh, ___ I'm a reb - el just for kicks, now. { I've been feel - ing it since
                                               { Let me kick it like it's

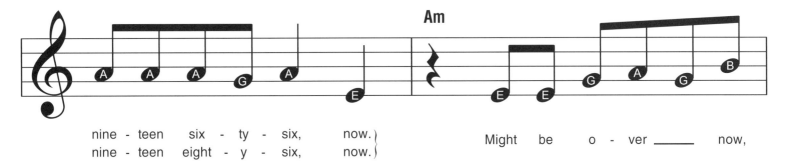

nine - teen six - ty - six, now. }
nine - teen eight - y - six, now. }   Might be o - ver ___ now,

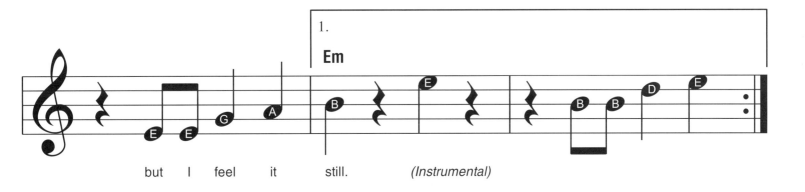

1.

but I feel it still.   (Instrumental)

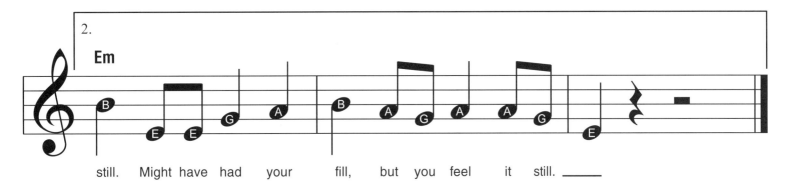

2.

still. Might have had your fill, but you feel it still. ___

Girls Like You

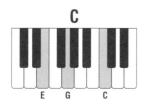
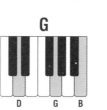
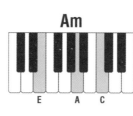
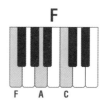

Words and Music by Adam Levine,
Brittany Hazzard, Jason Evigan,
Henry Walter and Gian Stone

Moderately fast

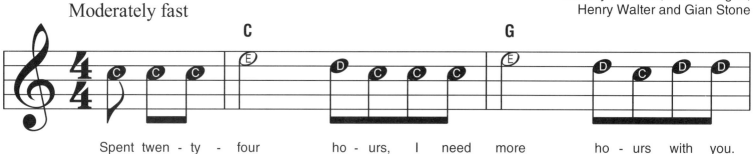

Spent twen-ty-four ho-urs, I need more ho-urs with you.

(Instrumental) You spent the week-end get-ting

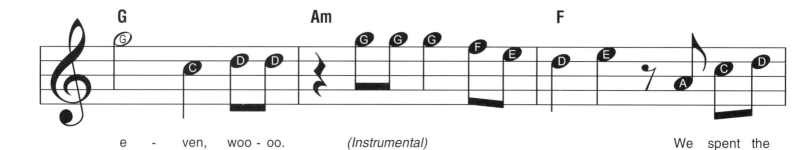

e-ven, woo-oo. (Instrumental) We spent the

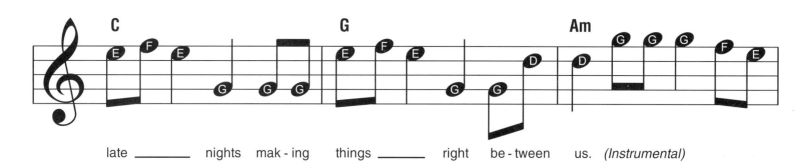

late _____ nights mak-ing things _____ right be-tween us. (Instrumental)

Happier

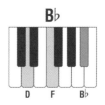
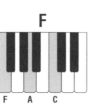

Words and Music by Marshmello,
Steve Mac and Dan Smith

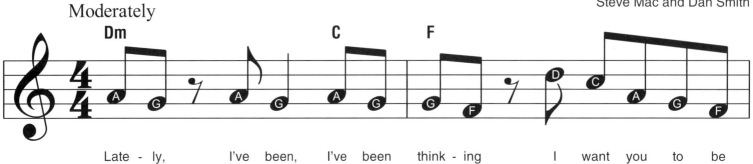

Moderately

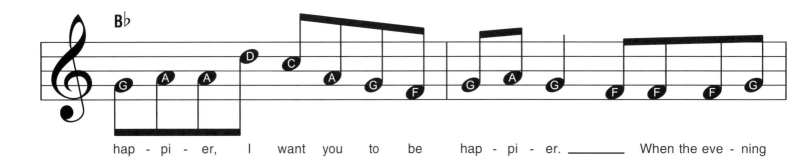

Late - ly, I've been, I've been think - ing I want you to be

hap - pi - er, I want you to be hap - pi - er. _____ When the eve - ning

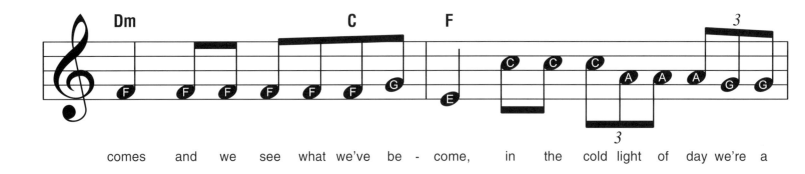

comes and we see what we've be - come, in the cold light of day we're a

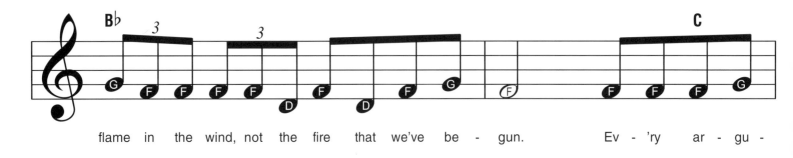

flame in the wind, not the fire that we've be - gun. Ev - 'ry ar - gu -

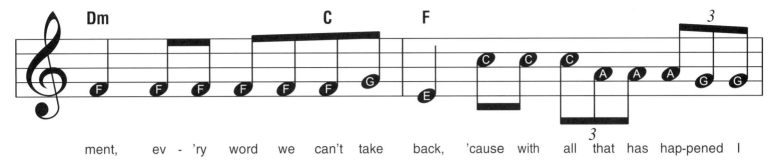

ment, ev - 'ry word we can't take back, 'cause with all that has hap-pened I

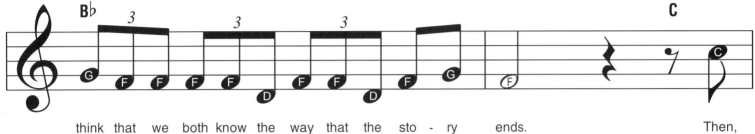

think that we both know the way that the sto - ry ends. Then,

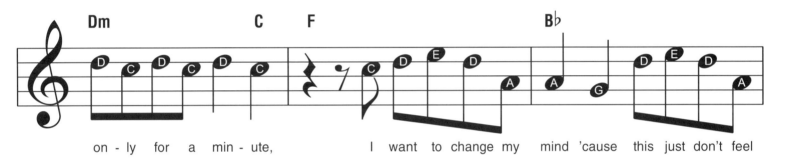

on - ly for a min - ute, I want to change my mind 'cause this just don't feel

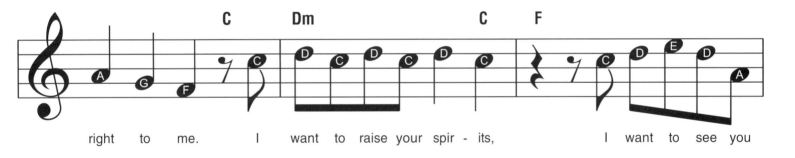

right to me. I want to raise your spir - its, I want to see you

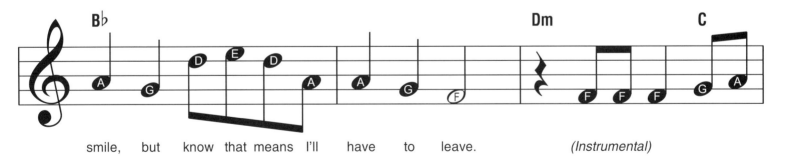

smile, but know that means I'll have to leave. *(Instrumental)*

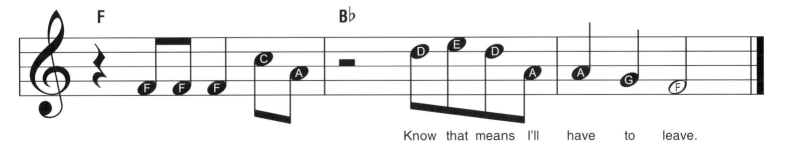

Know that means I'll have to leave.

Havana

Words and Music by Camila Cabello,
Louis Bell, Pharrell Williams,
Adam Feeney, Ali Tamposi,
Jeffery Lamar Williams, Brian Lee,
Andrew Wotman, Brittany Hazzard
and Kaan Gunesberk

With a Latin groove

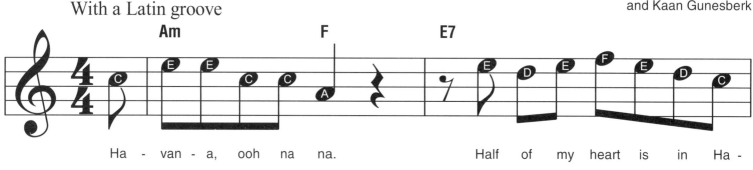

Ha - van - a, ooh na na. Half of my heart is in Ha -

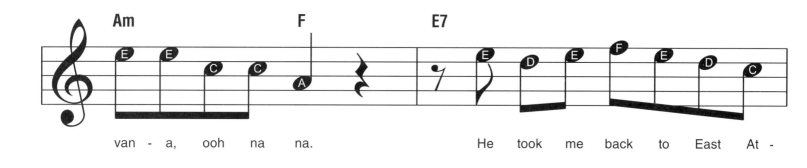

van - a, ooh na na. He took me back to East At -

lan - ta, na na na. Ah, but my heart is in Ha -

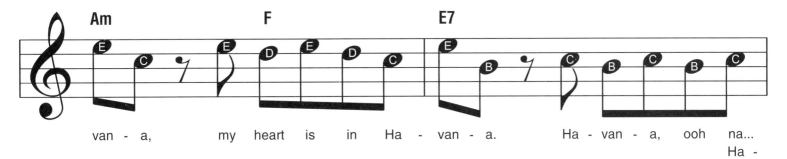

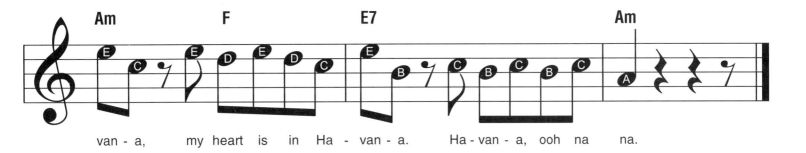

High Hopes

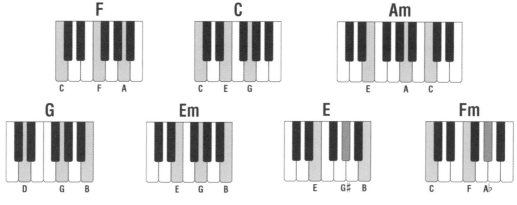

Words and Music by Brendon Urie,
Samuel Hollander, William Lobban Bean,
Jonas Jeberg, Jacob Sinclair,
Jenny Owen Youngs, Ilsey Juber,
Lauren Pritchard and Tayla Parx

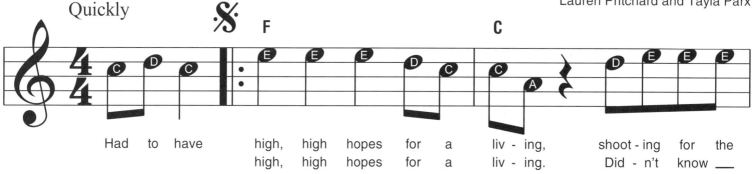

Had to have high, high hopes for a liv - ing, shoot - ing for the
high, high hopes for a liv - ing. Did - n't know ___

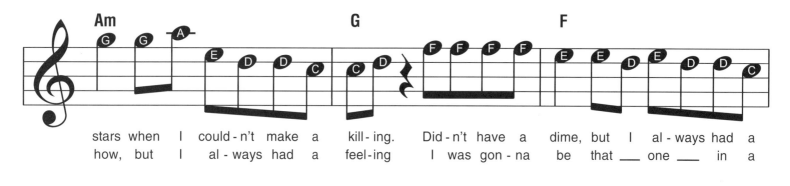

stars when I could - n't make a kill - ing. Did - n't have a dime, but I al - ways had a
how, but I al - ways had a feel - ing I was gon - na be that ___ one ___ in a

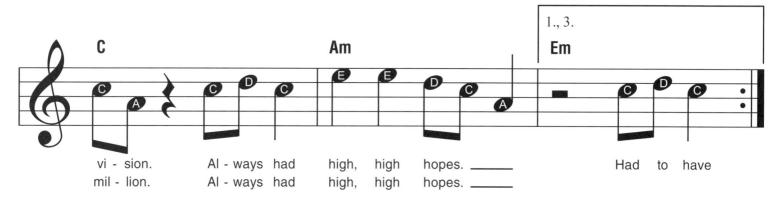

vi - sion. Al - ways had high, high hopes. _____
mil - lion. Al - ways had high, high hopes. _____ Had to have

If I Can't Have You

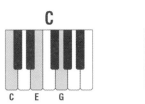
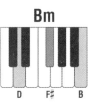
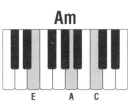
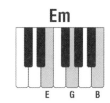

Words and Music by Shawn Mendes,
Teddy Geiger, Nate Mercereau
and Scott Harris

Upbeat Pop

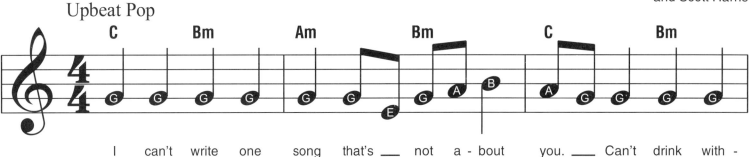

I can't write one song that's __ not a - bout you. __ Can't drink with -

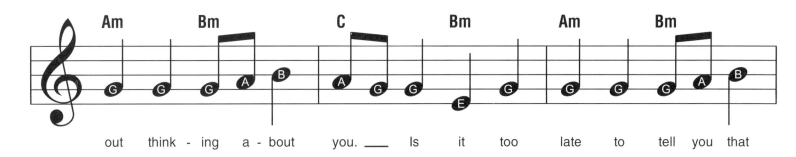

out think - ing a - bout you. __ Is it too late to tell you that

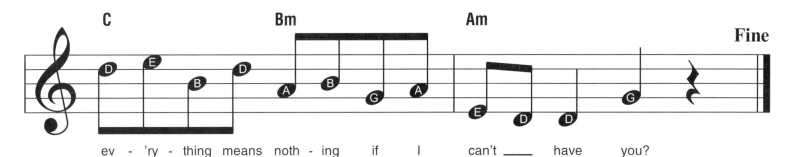

ev - 'ry - thing means noth - ing if I can't __ have you?

I'm in To - ron - to and I got this view, but I

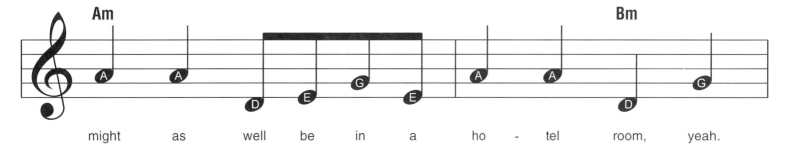

might as well be in a ho - tel room, yeah.

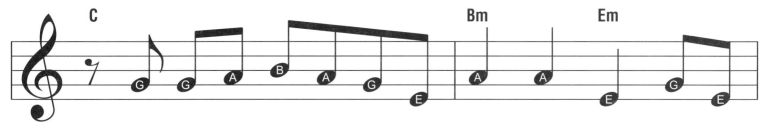

It does - n't mat - ter 'cause I'm so con - sumed, spend - ing

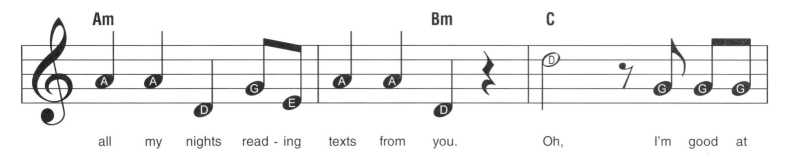

all my nights read - ing texts from you. Oh, I'm good at

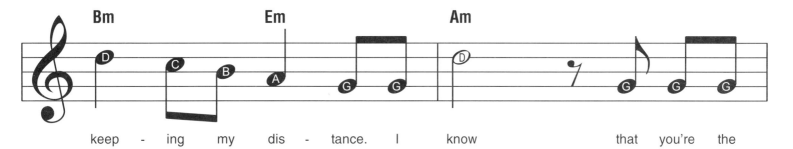

keep - ing my dis - tance. I know that you're the

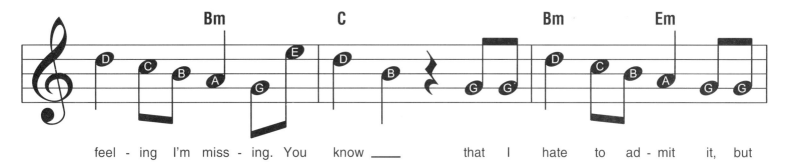

feel - ing I'm miss - ing. You know ____ that I hate to ad - mit it, but

D.C. al Fine
(Return to beginning
and play to Fine)

ev - 'ry - thing means noth - ing if I can't ____ have you.

Lovely

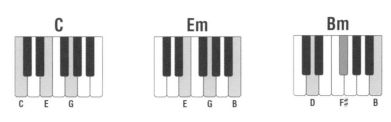

Words and Music by Billie Eilish O'Connell,
Finneas O'Connell and Khalid Robinson

Moderate Ballad

ME!

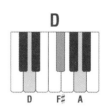

Words and Music by Taylor Swift,
Joel Little and Brendon Urie

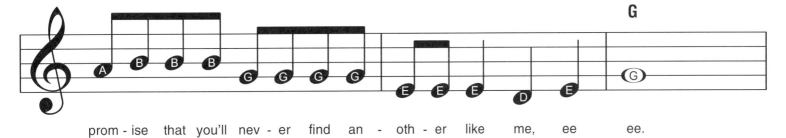

prom - ise that you'll nev - er find an - oth - er like me, ee ee.

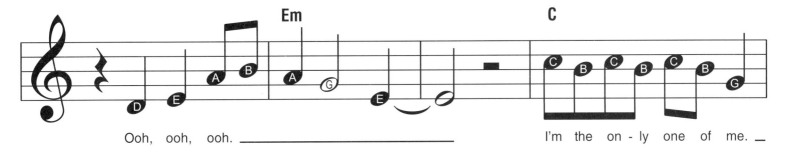

Ooh, ooh, ooh. _____ I'm the on - ly one of me. _

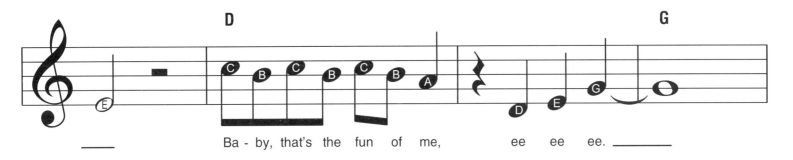

___ Ba - by, that's the fun of me, ee ee ee. _____

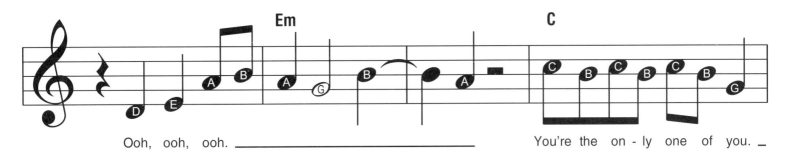

Ooh, ooh, ooh. _____ You're the on - ly one of you. _

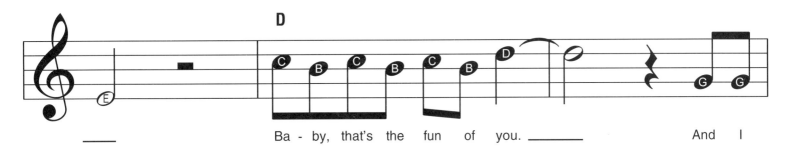

___ Ba - by, that's the fun of you. _____ And I

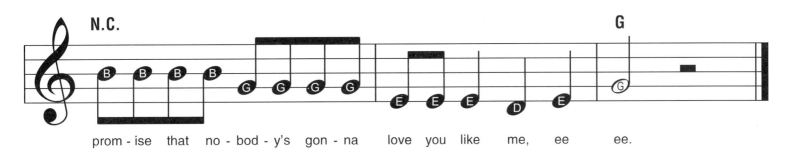

prom - ise that no - bod - y's gon - na love you like me, ee ee.

A Million Dreams
from THE GREATEST SHOWMAN

Words and Music by Benj Pasek
and Justin Paul

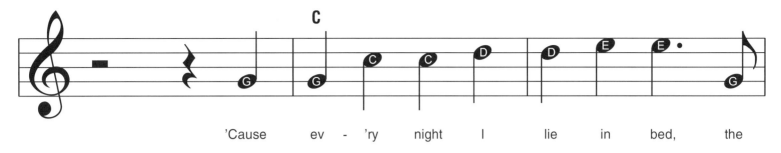

'Cause   ev - 'ry   night   I   lie   in   bed,   the

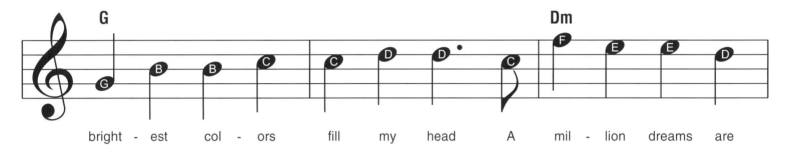

bright - est   col - ors   fill   my   head   A   mil - lion   dreams   are

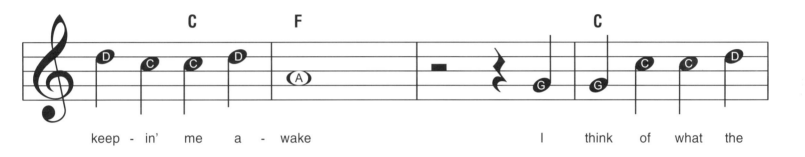

keep - in'   me   a - wake   I   think   of   what   the

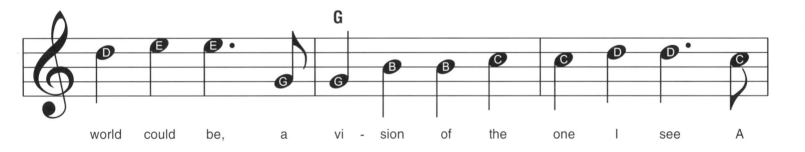

world   could   be,   a   vi - sion   of   the   one   I   see   A

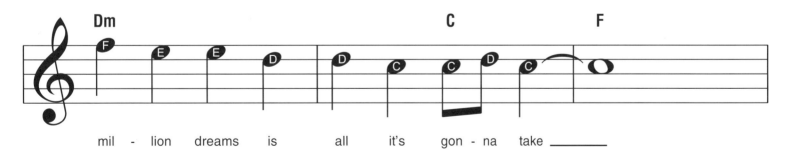

mil - lion   dreams   is   all   it's   gon - na   take _____

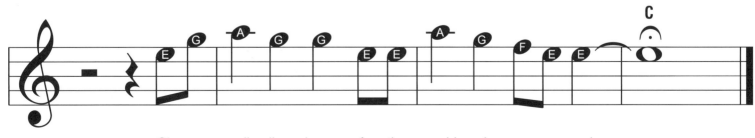

Oh,   a   mil - lion   dreams   for   the   world   we're   gon - na   make _____

Old Town Road
(Remix)

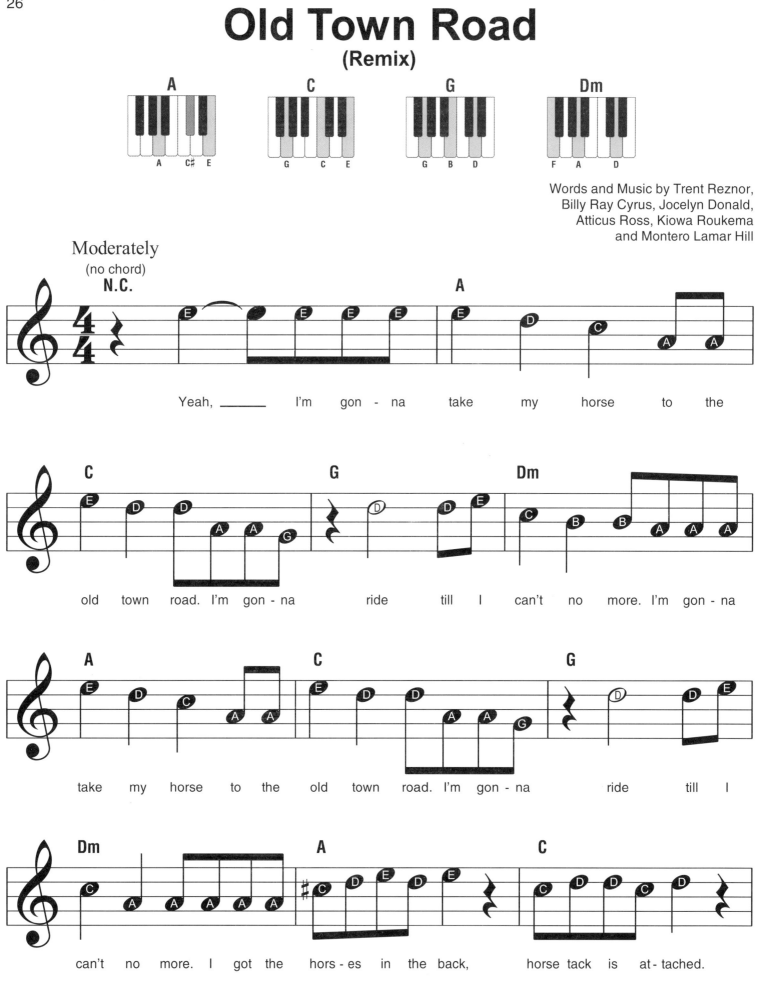

Words and Music by Trent Reznor,
Billy Ray Cyrus, Jocelyn Donald,
Atticus Ross, Kiowa Roukema
and Montero Lamar Hill

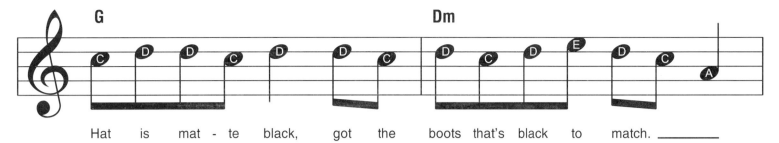

Hat is mat - te black, got the boots that's black to match. _____

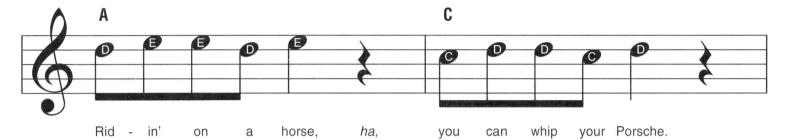

Rid - in' on a horse, *ha,* you can whip your Porsche.

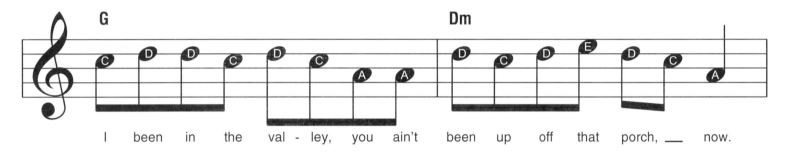

I been in the val - ley, you ain't been up off that porch, ___ now.

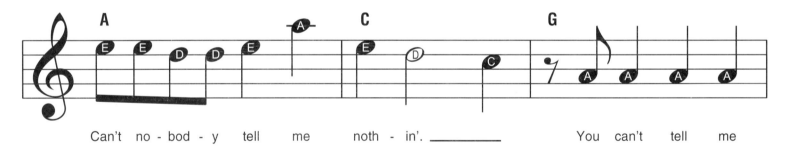

Can't no-bod - y tell me noth - in'. _____ You can't tell me

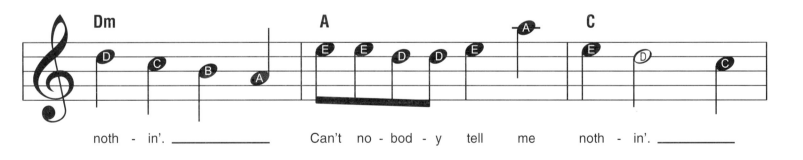

noth - in'. _____ Can't no-bod - y tell me noth - in'. _____

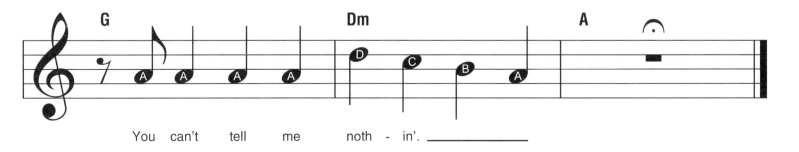

You can't tell me noth - in'. _____

Perfect

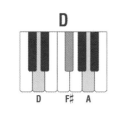
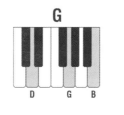
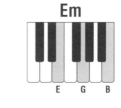
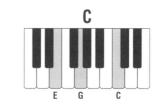

Words and Music by
Ed Sheeran

'Cause we were just kids when we fell _____ in _____
kiss _____ me _____

love, not know-ing what _____ it was. I will not
slow. Your heart is all _____ I own. And in your

give you _____ up this time. _____
eyes, you're _____ hold - ing

Dar - ling, just mine. Ba - by, _____

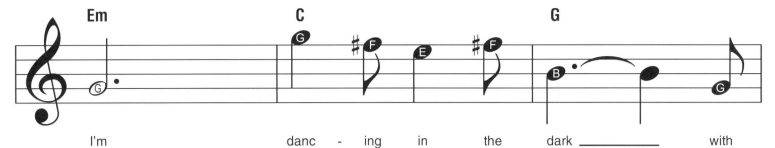

I'm danc - ing in the dark _____ with

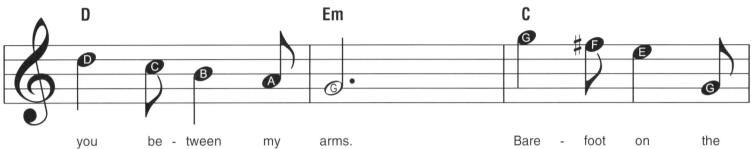

you be - tween my arms. Bare - foot on the

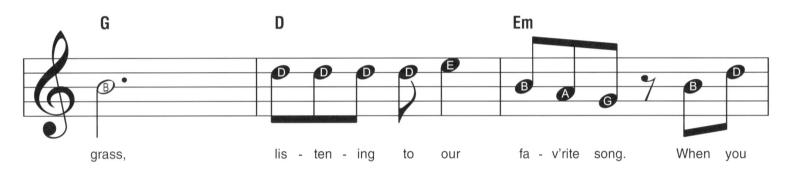

grass, lis - ten - ing to our fa - v'rite song. When you

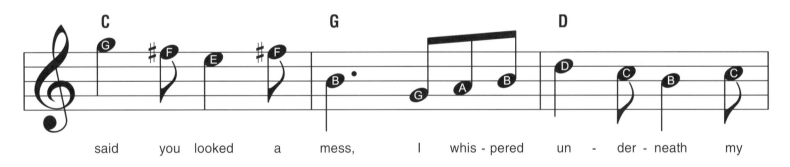

said you looked a mess, I whis - pered un - der - neath my

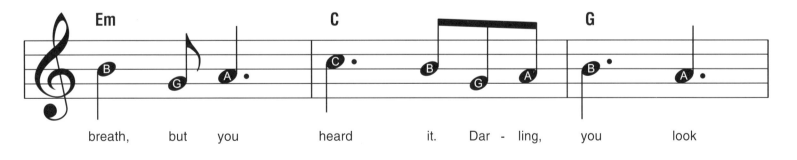

breath, but you heard it. Dar - ling, you look

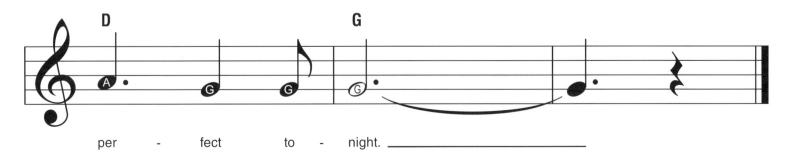

per - fect to - night. _____

Shallow
from A STAR IS BORN

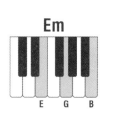
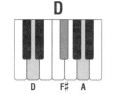
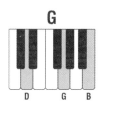
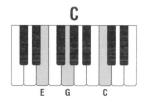
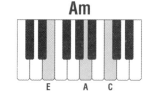

Words and Music by Stefani Germanotta,
Mark Ronson, Andrew Wyatt
and Anthony Rossomando

Moderately

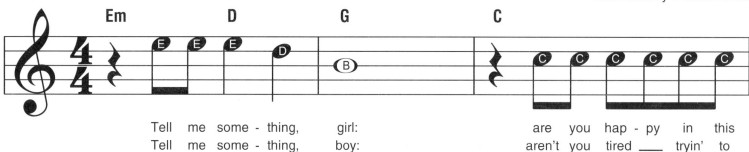

Tell me some - thing, girl: are you hap - py in this
Tell me some - thing, boy: aren't you tired ___ tryin' to

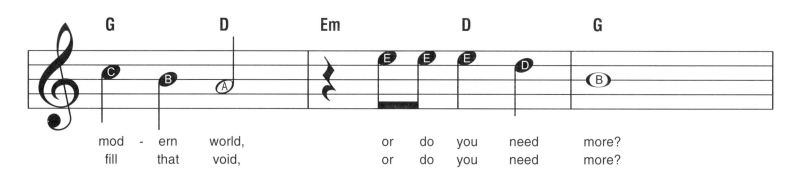

mod - ern world,   or do you need more?
fill that void,   or do you need more?

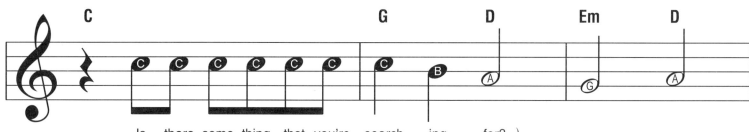

Is there some - thing that you're search - ing for? }
Ain't it hard keep - ing it so hard - core? }   I'm fall -

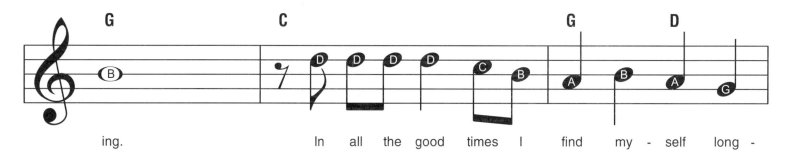

ing.   In all the good times I find my - self long -

ing   for   change,   and in the bad times I fear my - self.

Am   D   G   D

I'm off   the deep end.   Watch as I dive in.   I'll nev - er meet the
Crash through the sur - face, where they can't hurt us. We're far from the shal - low

Em   Am   D

ground. _____   In   the shal, - al, - shal, - al - low,
now. _____

G   D   Em   Am

In   the shal, - shal - al, - al, - al - low.   In   the shal, - al, -

D   G   D   Em

shal, - al - low, we're far from the shal - low now.

Someone You Loved

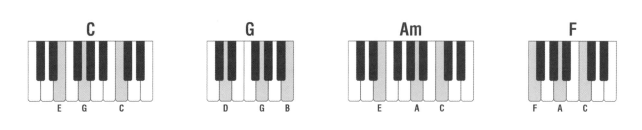

Words and Music by Lewis Capaldi,
Benjamin Kohn, Peter Kelleher,
Thomas Barnes and Samuel Roman

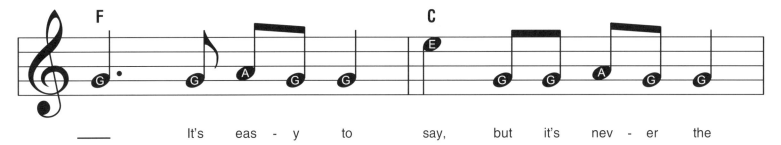

It's eas - y to say, but it's nev - er the

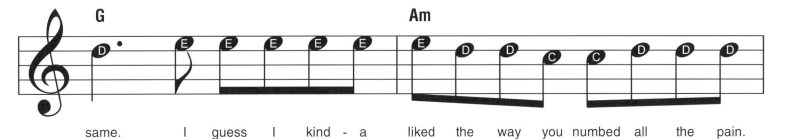

same. I guess I kind - a liked the way you numbed all the pain.

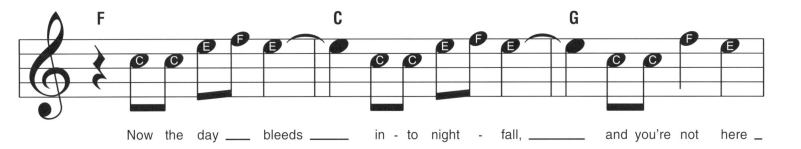

Now the day ___ bleeds ___ in - to night - fall, ___ and you're not here _

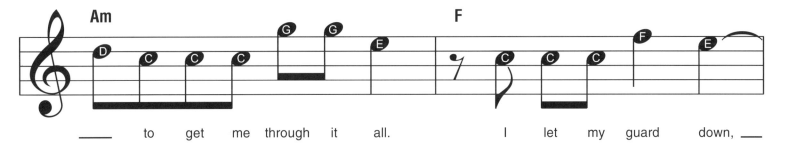

___ to get me through it all. I let my guard down, ___

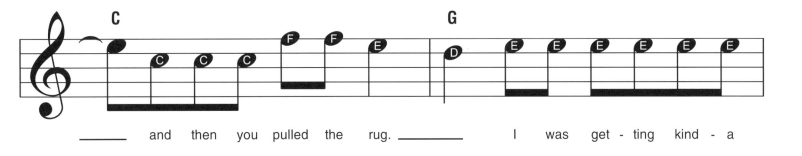

___ and then you pulled the rug. ___ I was get - ting kind - a

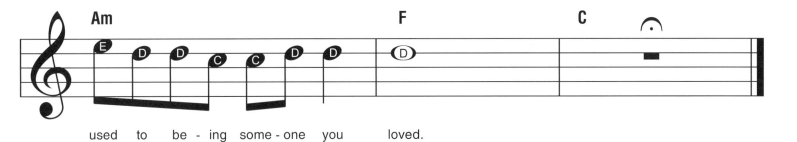

used to be - ing some - one you loved.

Something Just Like This

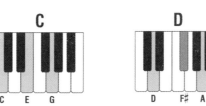
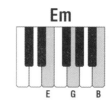

Words and Music by Andrew Taggart,
Chris Martin, Guy Berryman,
Jonny Buckland and Will Champion

Moderately
(no chord)

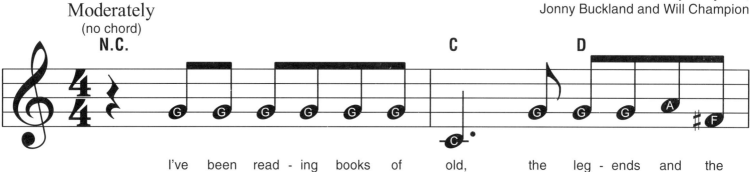

I've been read-ing books of old, the leg-ends and the

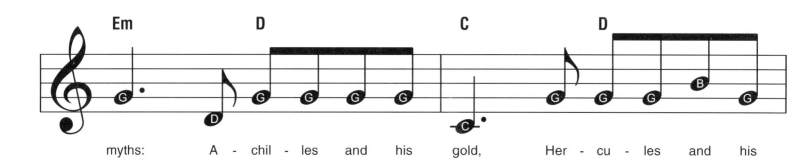

myths: A-chil-les and his gold, Her-cu-les and his

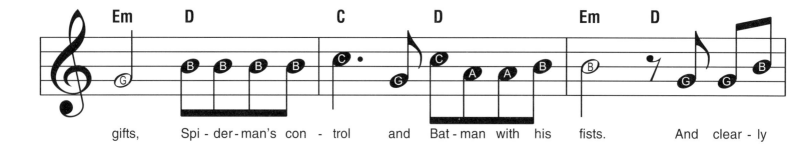

gifts, Spi-der-man's con-trol and Bat-man with his fists. And clear-ly

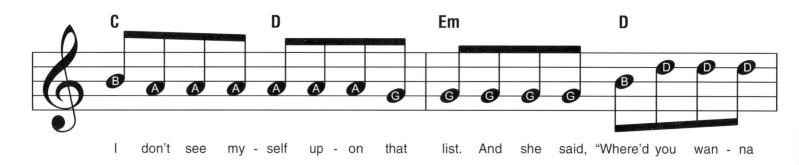

I don't see my-self up-on that list. And she said, "Where'd you wan-na

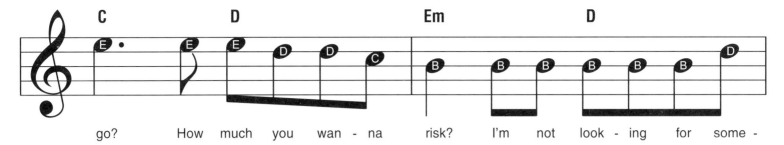

go? How much you wan-na risk? I'm not look-ing for some-

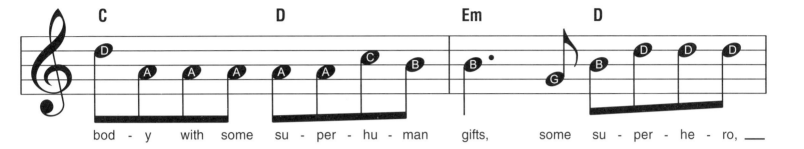

bod-y with some su-per-hu-man gifts, some su-per-he-ro, ___

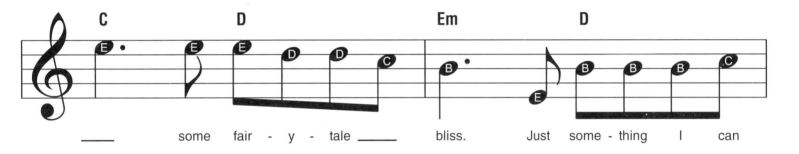

___ some fair-y-tale ___ bliss. Just some-thing I can

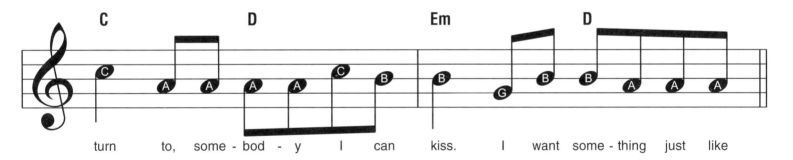

turn to, some-bod-y I can kiss. I want some-thing just like

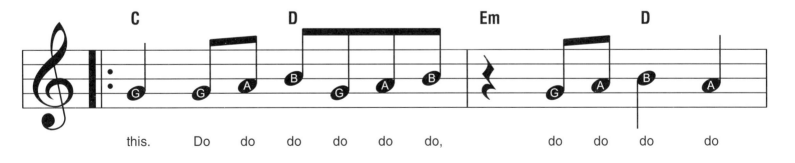

this. Do do do do do do, do do do do

do, do do do do do do. Oh, I want some-thing just like this.

Sucker

Sunflower
from SPIDER-MAN: INTO THE SPIDER-VERSE

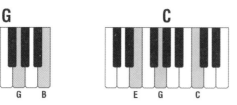
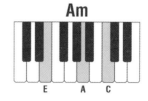

Words and Music by Austin Richard Post,
Carl Austin Rosen, Khalif Brown,
Carter Lang, Louis Bell
and Billy Walsh

Need-less to say, I keep her in check. She was all bad-bad, nev-er-the-less.

Call-ing it quits now, ba-by, I'm a wreck. Crash at my place, ba-by, you're a wreck.

Need-less to say, I'm keep-ing her in check. She was all bad-bad, nev-er-the-less.

Call-ing it quits now, ba-by, I'm a wreck. Crash at my place, ba-by, you're a wreck.

Sweet but Psycho

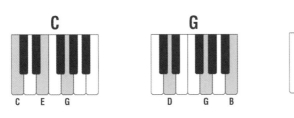

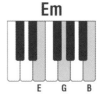

Words and Music by Amanda Koci,
Andreas Haukeland, William Lobban Bean,
Henry Walter and Madison Love

Moderately fast

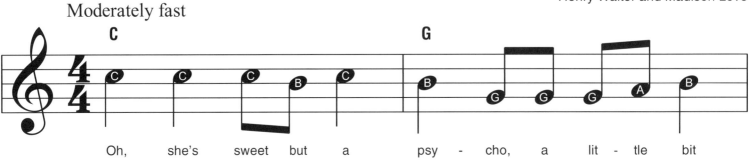
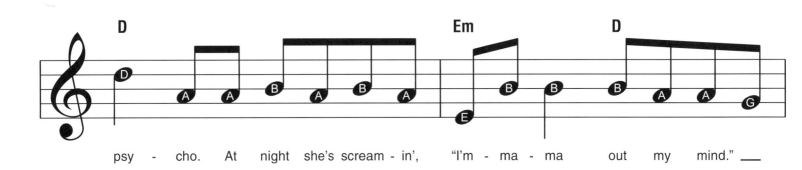
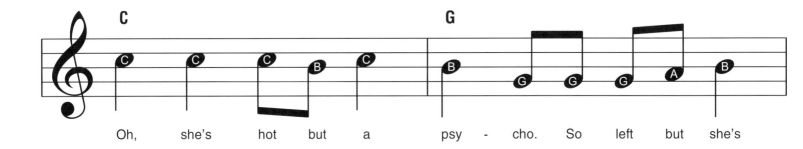
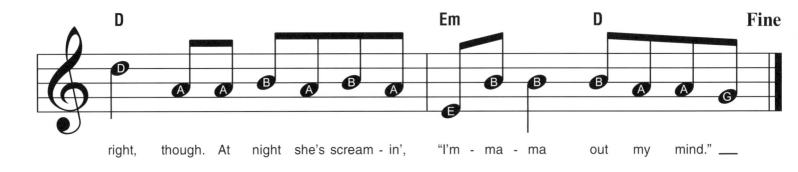

Oh, she's sweet but a psy-cho, a lit-tle bit psy-cho. At night she's scream-in', "I'm-ma-ma out my mind." ___

Oh, she's hot but a psy-cho. So left but she's right, though. At night she's scream-in', "I'm-ma-ma out my mind." ___

Without Me

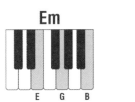
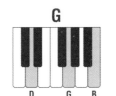

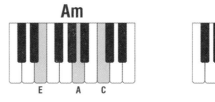
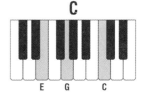

Words and Music by Ashley Frangipane,
Brittany Amaradio, Miles Ale,
Justin Timberlake, Scott Storch,
Louis Bell, Amy Allen
and Timothy Mosley

Moderate groove

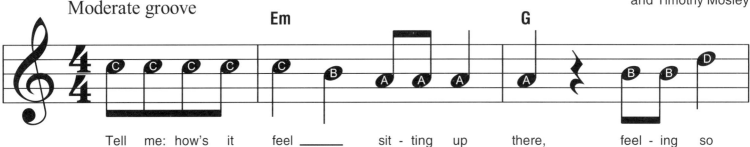

Tell me: how's it feel _____ sit - ting up there, feel - ing so

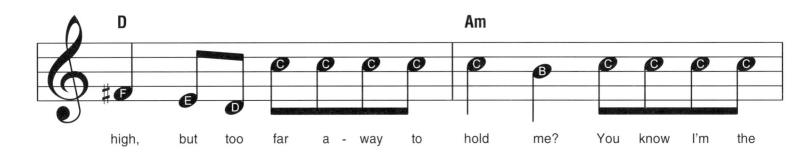

high, but too far a - way to hold me? You know I'm the

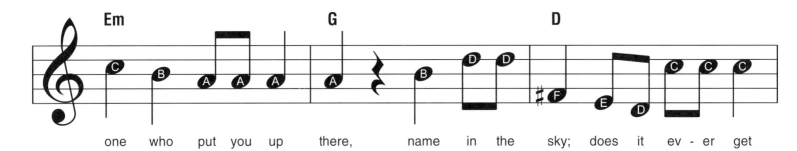

one who put you up there, name in the sky; does it ev - er get

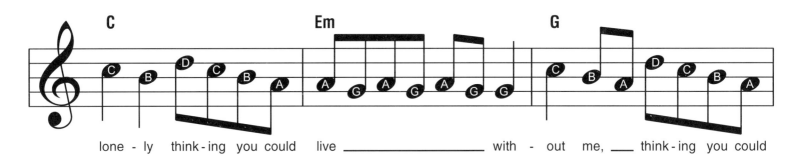

lone - ly think - ing you could live _____ with - out me, _____ think - ing you could

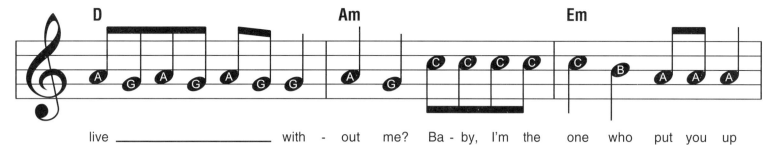

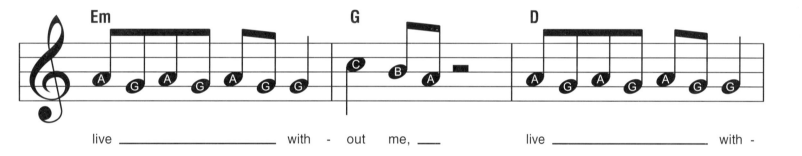

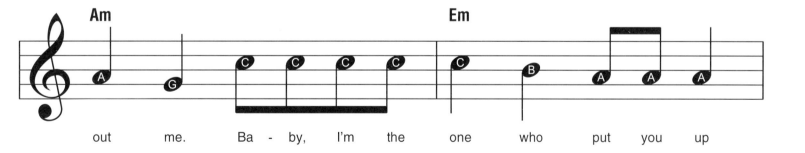

You Are the Reason

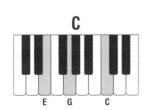
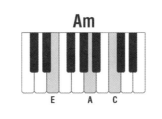
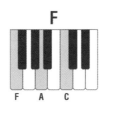
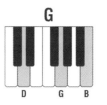
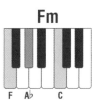

Words and Music by Calum Scott,
Corey Sanders and Jonathan Maguire

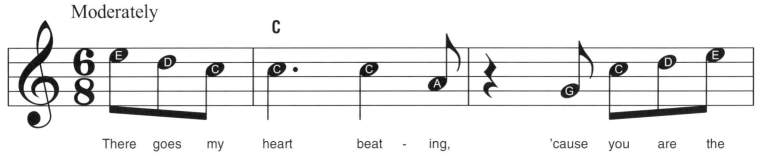

There goes my heart beat - ing, 'cause you are the

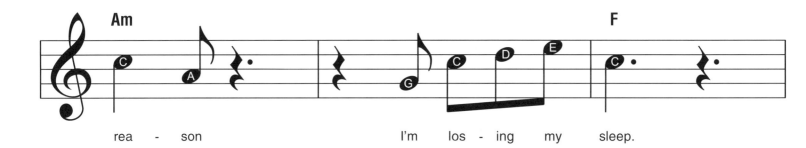

rea - son I'm los - ing my sleep.

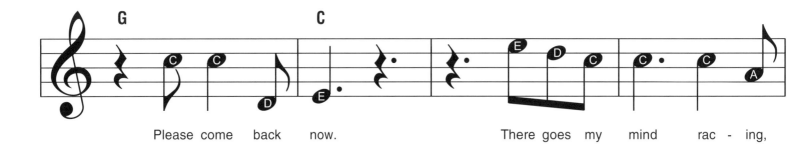

Please come back now. There goes my mind rac - ing,

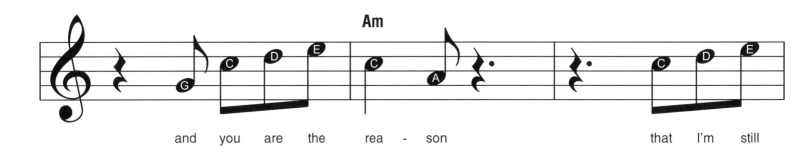

and you are the rea - son that I'm still

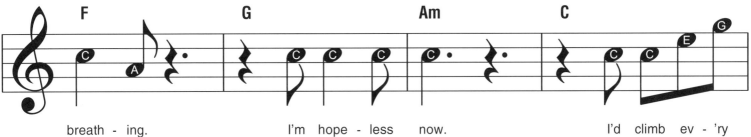

breath - ing.   I'm hope - less now.   I'd climb ev - 'ry

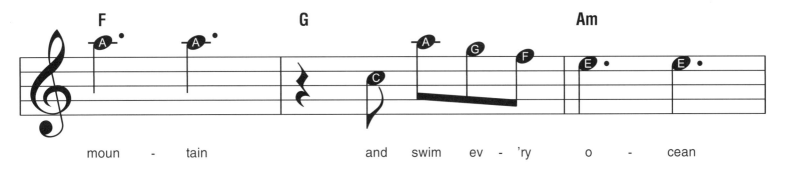

moun - tain   and swim ev - 'ry o - cean

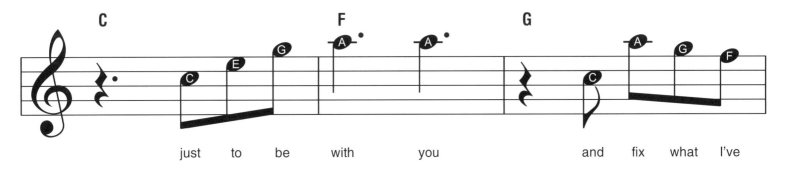

just to be with you   and fix what I've

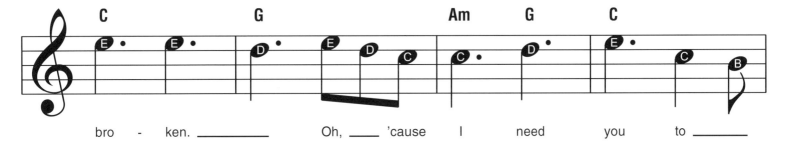

bro - ken. _____ Oh, ___ 'cause I need you to _____

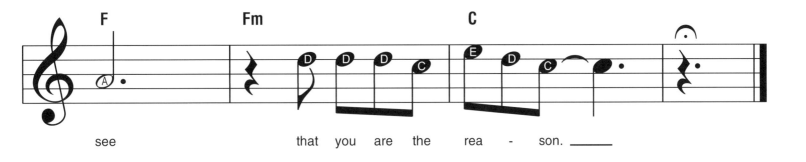

see   that you are the rea - son. _____

You Say

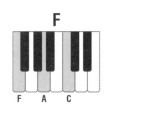
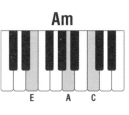
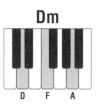
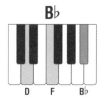

Words and Music by Lauren Daigle,
Jason Ingram and Paul Mabury

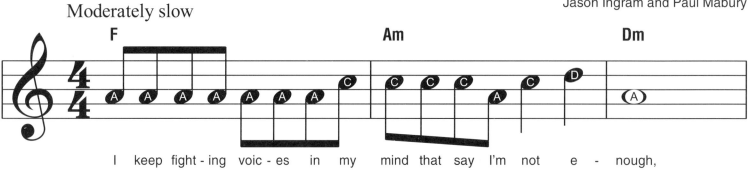

I keep fight-ing voic-es in my mind that say I'm not e - nough,

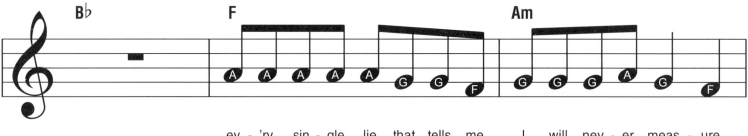

ev - 'ry sin - gle lie that tells me I will nev - er meas - ure

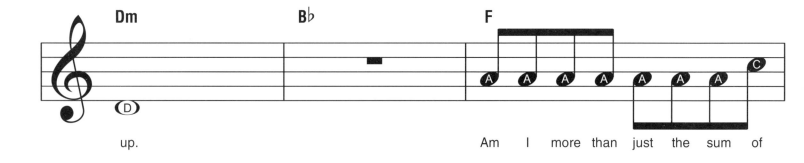

up. Am I more than just the sum of

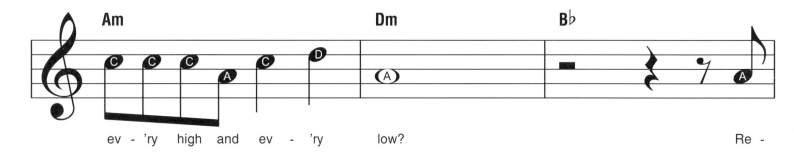

ev - 'ry high and ev - 'ry low? Re -

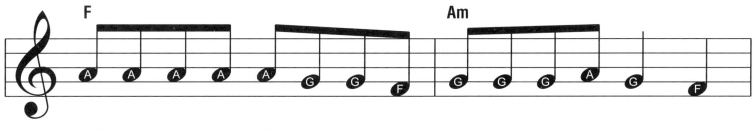

mind me once a - gain just who I am, be - cause I need to

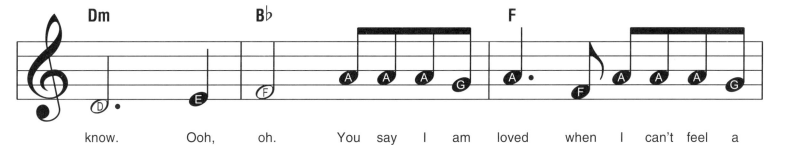

know.   Ooh,   oh.   You   say   I   am   loved   when   I   can't   feel   a

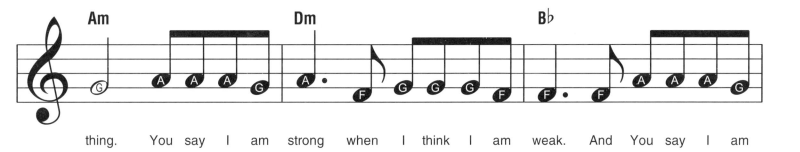

thing.   You   say   I   am   strong   when   I   think   I   am   weak.   And   You   say   I   am

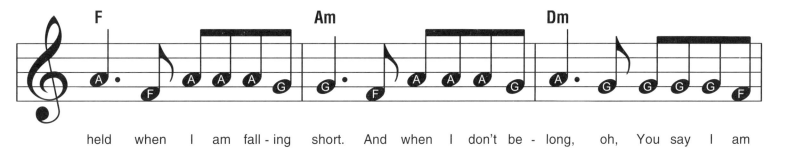

held   when   I   am   fall - ing   short.   And   when   I   don't   be - long,   oh,   You   say   I   am

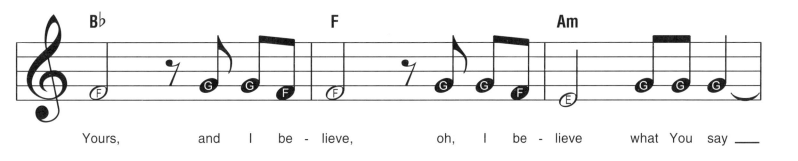

Yours,   and   I   be - lieve,   oh,   I   be - lieve   what   You   say ___

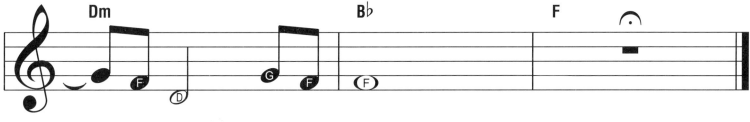

_____   of   me.   I   be - lieve.